JUST A
MOMENT

JUST A MOMENT

First Edition November 1983

Second Edition June 1995

ISBN 1-886872-00-7

Published by the Brahma Kumaris World Spiritual University,
Literature Department, 65 Pound Lane, London NW10 2HH UK

There are Brahma Kumaris Centres in over 62 countries worldwide.

Printed by Waterside Litho, Chesham UK

Available in other languages

C O N T E N T S

PREFACE

This booklet is the result of a radio programme "Just a Moment" broadcast daily by Garfield King on the radio station "Voice of Barbados." An experienced teacher of meditation, these selected scripts are based on his practical experiences and understanding of spirituality. For him, spirituality has become a powerful tool for the enrichment of life and the resolution of conflict. The text was compiled by students of the Brahma Kumaris World Spiritual University, St. Michael, Barbados.

This short collection of thoughts will go far, I am sure, in bringing peace to every soul that takes time to study it. Readers may have heard Garfield King's voice on morning radio, taking a moment to set us on course for the day; or will have read his script in the daily paper. This collection of thoughts may help you along the path of spiritual development if you take just a moment.

Ridley Greene, Senior Assistant Editor, The Nation

The poet John Clare once questioned: "What is this life if, full of care, we have no time to stand and stare?"

Garfield King, of the Brahma Kumaris Raja Yoga Centre, in this interesting and thought-provoking series, encourages us to take just a moment to stop and reflect on the quality of our daily lives.

Julian Rogers, Voice of Barbados

Let the drama of life unfold itself

Being a good organiser, I have planned my day. I've listed all the activities and schedules for the next 24 hours. I have a lot to accomplish. I am not one for being caught up in trivial matters. I am methodical and efficient with my time. After all, time is valuable and should be utilised wisely. So, I have made my plans for the day.

And what a day! From early morning, everything seems to be conspiring to make a mockery of my plan, of my efficiency. I have been confronted with many unexpected circumstances, demanding my time and energy, keeping me away from the "real", or so I think, things that concern me. Yes, life is full of its uncertainties and my best-made plans are sometimes made useless and ineffective.

The best way to maintain a state of equilibrium and always remain calm is to become an observer. Step aside a little and watch the scenes of the drama. Even though I am an actor in the scene and even though I have to enact my role in these events, I can develop a state of conscious detachment that helps me to deal more effectively with the situation. Being too close, I take my role in the drama for the real thing. I become confused, intimidated and, worst of all, lose my cool – my equilibrium.

Try to think one pure thought every day

I am what I think. The mind is constantly occupied in the thought process, and it is virtually impossible to have a vacant yet alive mind. Without doubt, my entire world has been created by my thoughts. Sometimes the results of these thoughts are manifested immediately and sometimes results take a longer period to come into the practical. However, the fact remains that thoughts, when given constant energy and attention, will come into practical. They are the basis for all my actions.

If I must think, and if by thinking I create the world around me, negative or positive, through actions, negative or positive, wouldn't it then make sense for me to think the very highest of thoughts, the purest of thoughts, so that the world I create would be of that corresponding quality–high, noble and pure?

And what is a pure thought? Aren't all thoughts pure simply by nature of being a thought? A pure thought is one that is free from all the vices such as ego, hatred, pride, jealousy, greed or anger. A pure thought, when transferred into action, enriches the creator as well as the creation. It is an energy that is formed at the most exalted levels of self-respect, but extends far beyond the self, making everything it touches exalted.

Pure thoughts are becoming sadly rare, as is evidenced by the world I have created around me. The pollution in all areas speaks of impurity within the thought processes.

Eternal laws

Whatever is new must become old. Everything passes through this process.

I look back into time. In a second or less, my thoughts take me to a place far away both in time and space; for a moment, I relive the scenes of the past, and then I come back to the present, with a smile on my face. The smile quickly changes, and I sigh when I realise how different the present is. "What has happened? Why couldn't it be like that still?"

There is a simple law which states, "Whatever is new must become old". It is always good to know the laws. I may not think that they make much sense, I may even disagree with them; but some laws just cannot be changed, so I learn to live with them and follow them. There is no point in asking questions as to why, how, when, where and what. It doesn't matter. The point is that I should understand the laws of living and take benefit from them. Here are three such laws that won't change and are worth remembering:

1. Whatever I sow, I will reap.

2. Whatever is new will become old.

3. Whatever I don't use, I lose.

See problems as opportunities

When a problem comes, do I panic or do I see it as a challenge? Sometimes the whole world seems like a problem; sometimes I need to create problems so as to keep myself busy. A problem is only a problem when I call it a problem. A situation is only as difficult as I want it to be.

Difficulties and disappointments are the events which lead me to maturity. After all, wisdom does not necessarily come with age; it is the gift of experience.

I have the tendency to imagine that my problems are greater and more important than anyone else's. It is in fact a subtle form of of ego; the feeling that "my problem is worse than your problem, so you must give me regard".

More often I am so confused and clouded that I cannot see a clear way out of a given problem, with the result that fear and tension build up, and I become irritable and filled with self-pity. In that frame of mind the smallest obstacle becomes huge.

I keep running away from situations that I find disagreeable; and the further I run away from a problem, the more difficult it is to resolve.

Talking to God

Very often in my quiet moments, my moments of reflection and self-examination, I realise that certain things I have done were wrong.

I have caused sorrow to someone, either through thought, word or action; I may have been keeping someone at a distance, giving them the cold treatment; I may have satisfied my desire at the expense of others, or I may have been living a life of deceit.

I feel remorse, regret, and I promise to change, to improve myself. But what about those past actions? They seem to be a burden on my head and, the more I recall them, the heavier they seem to get. It is at such times that I can experience God as my friend; the one I can talk to and share personal things with; the one who will forgive and direct me and be my guide. I do not have to make an appointment to talk to God, and I am not embarrassed to disclose my secrets to God.

It is true that I have to reap the fruit of the seeds I sow, but with knowledge of this truth and help from God, strength and courage increase.

I have a friend who is always there, not only in times of distress and sorrow, but in times of happiness too.

The greatest instrument—thought

The most powerful instrument that mankind possesses is thought power. I look at the physical world and observe the devastating power of atomic and nuclear weapons. A nuclear warhead the size of a cricket ball can wipe out a whole city, even an entire country; and yet who made such devices? Man or, to be more accurate, the mind of man. And which is the most powerful, creator or creation?

The one who creates has the greater power. Some say that our thoughts are more powerful than nuclear weapons. So what has gone wrong? Why can I not use this power of the mind to benefit myself and others?

Firstly, I have forgotten that I ever had this power; and secondly, I no longer have the ability to harness and make use of it.

I have forgotten that I am a soul and have developed the false concept of myself as being merely a body; and, in so doing, I immediately limit myself to all that is physical. However, life does not exist only on a physical level.

For example, I have to think, remember, decide, experience, judge, learn and a long list of other functions that the body itself cannot perform. Can the body think; can it make decisions? What part of my body has memory or the ability to judge? Is it my leg, my elbow, my nose?

It is the soul that performs these tasks.

*P*atience comes from a peaceful mind

I have become conditioned and programmed into immediate responses. I flick switches, turn knobs, and something or the other comes into action. When a piece of equipment fails to respond, I get annoyed.

I do not like to wait. I become easily impatient. Because of this impatience I lose out on the full benefits of life. I become angry and hateful until finally I am dissatisfied and discontented with life.

Where is my patience buried? Why is it so difficult to be patient in situations? Is it my conceit or ego that submerges my patience, or is it my over-eagerness to attain and acquire that destabilises me and makes me disturbed and impatient?

Patience is a reflection of the peaceful mind. My peaceful mind is able to cope with all situations without becoming disturbed and agitated. It calmly accepts the resolution of circumstances and, with this patience, acquires the power to deal with all situations.

$\mathcal{I}s$ patience a virtue or is it a hassle?

Is patience a virtue or is it a hassle? Does it mean to be subservient, relegated and docile?

Patience has little space in the fast-moving materialistic world. "I must make things happen";"I must make hay while the sun shines". These are old wise sayings which have been totally misinterpreted to imply that people must not wait unnecessarily.

Do I think that I must bulldoze my way by whatever means possible to make things happen at my rate of progress? In doing this I not only lose my patience, but also all my controlling powers such as the power to tolerate, the power to adjust, the power to co-operate and the power to discriminate.

When I lose my patience I lose control. This control ranges from the very gross to the most subtle levels. From this perspective, then, patience becomes a powerful weapon with which to challenge the dramas of life.

Feel free to give a helping hand

People feel that if they co-operate, they have earned a right to the reward. And there lies one reason for lack of co-operation–greed. If I can appreciate the joys of sharing, then I can experience true happiness.

I often hear people say, "I was doing my best, but so-and-so refused to co-operate, so why should I bother?" If someone is being unco-operative, I must increase my co-operation. I cannot sit doing nothing forever. Things have to be done sooner or later. If I begin, others will definitely follow. If I develop the habit of waiting for others to do, I will be left behind. And if when I am doing, there is no ego, just love and sweetness, this will inspire others to lend a hand.

I once saw a symbol for co-operation: many hands each using one finger to lift a mountain. Today I can take this thought with me. Rather than feel that I am competing with anyone, it is much better to feel that I am giving co-operation to all.

Silence is golden

Silence is a power which can take either a positive or a negative form. If I understand the nature of this power, I can use it in a beneficial way. There are two levels of silence: physical and mental.

Physical silence refers to the absence of sound. People are normally fearful of this silence because it suggests absence of life or company - just as when a person dies, there is total silence afterwards.

In comparison to this, mental silence is the absence of wasteful thinking. Wasteful thinking refers to negative thoughts. In contrast to this, positive thinking refers to thoughts which benefit the self as well as others. Constant positive thinking creates the virtue of serenity and stabilises me as well as my companions. This type of silence power is like a fragrance which fills a room. It is an unspoken language which can cross all barriers.

This silence is not a blank state or the silence of someone sulking, but rather the deep comfort and joy one can experience after being relieved of some pressure or burden.

Start the day well

Is it a very good morning? If the day begins with my thoughts scattered in many different directions or with anxiety about a situation to occur later in the day, it will prove difficult to maintain a positive attitude throughout the day. This is because my first series of thoughts in the morning sets the pattern for the whole day. If I do not use the early morning hours to sort out my thoughts, what other time in the day will I find to perform such a task?

To sort out thoughts there needs to be clarity in the intellect. I have to check and see if there are any wasteful thoughts and, if there are, then remove them by adopting a positive and pure attitude. If there are wasteful thoughts, and I try to battle with them, it is as if I am giving them life and strength. Wasteful and negative thoughts are created by a weak mind; they have no real foundation; they are only paper tigers. Instead of battling with them I should simply create pure, positive thoughts which will automatically displace the weak, wasteful ones. For example, instead of thinking, "I must not get angry, I must not get angry", which is negative conditioning, it is better to think, "I understand why they behave that way".

Look for the virtues in others

Today I am going to experiment and make a genuine effort to see at least one virtue in every person with whom I come into contact. I know that no one is perfect, so why dwell on anyone's defects? If I actively search for goodness in others it can be found. There is not a single human being in existence who does not possess at least one virtue. I will at least see that and look at each person with that particular virtue in mind. This has a great effect.

If I am thinking about someone's weakness or defect, I may become uneasy and irritated. I feel annoyed and wonder, "Why does this person have to be this way?" and "Why does this person do such-and-such a thing all the time?" On the other hand, if I am thinking about someone's good qualities, I begin to feel lightness and easiness within my mind. Then I am influenced by the sweetness of that person. The world is a variety show, and the role of each one is different.

Like musical notes, people are different

When I pick up a guitar to play, I will need to use two hands. With one hand I will hold down a chord. Each finger will be holding down a different note behind a particular fret. With my other hand I will strum or pluck the strings. Six strings all vibrating at their own frequency, creating their own individual sound. However, it is that very difference in the sound of each note that creates the end result of a beautiful tonal image. Sounds that dance and glide on the eardrum.

I live, and yet it seems that I wish to renounce that music of life. I find it so difficult to accept the differences between people. I want everyone to be as I am, act as I act, think as I think or even believe what I believe. Can that be possible?

Have I ever heard guitarists play only one note in the whole of their musical career?

If people were exactly the same there would be no growth. There would be nothing new to stimulate our intellects and inspire us towards deeper thinking.

Why worry, have faith

No matter how much I worry about a problem, will my worried mind reach a solution?

It is very unlikely. What will probably happen is that I will become upset and frustrated, and feel heavy and burdened. I may lose sleep, lose appetite, lose everything - probably all I will gain is an ulcer, a wrinkled brow and tension.

I can make quite a hobby out of worrying. I worry about the noise and then complain when it is too quiet. I worry about having too many sunny dry spells and then complain when it rains. I may even be worried about worrying too much. It is essential to take an honest interest in what goes on around me, and of course it is always wise to analyse a situation and take the necessary precautions to avoid being influenced by anything negative. However, when all is said and done, my tense and burdened mind will not be able to function clearly enough to arrive at a suitable solution to a problem.

Maybe I should just do the best that I can and beyond that leave it in the hands of God. To have faith in the self, faith in God and faith in God's plan is a sure way to remain clear and free of burdens.

Remembering and forgetting

I make promises to myself, to others and even to God, with honesty in my heart and real sincerity. But then time passes and I find that some promises are kept and others are not. When I check I find that two factors contribute to my change of heart. It could be that circumstances changed, or that I as an individual changed. What was important to me yesterday is somehow not so important today, and so promises are broken and forgotten.

Some promises made to the self and to God, if kept, will improve me and in turn the world. I need to remind myself of such promises daily and have the determined thought to stick to them. This requires effort. Even if I make promises with tears in my eyes and from the bottom of my heart, time has a way of cooling things down, making me forget.

The path of progress is really like a pilgrimage of remembrance. It is necessary to remind myself as much as possible of the goal to improve and the one who can help me achieve that goal - God. In fact, the more I remember God, the more I can experience guidance, protection, liberation and friendship.

The influence of gossip

I cannot afford to overlook the influence that other people have on me. I hear of cases where people quarrel, fight and even commit murder because they are influenced by gossip, influenced by the words of others. To what extent do I check that I am not being influenced by gossip?

Negativity in the mind is like poison. Negative thoughts are the seeds of negative actions. It might seem like a simple everyday occurrence - my friend tells me in the strictest confidence that such a person is like this and does so-and-so. I listen and accept without question because of the friendship. My attitudes and actions now become influenced by my friend's words, and I find myself acting and reacting in accordance with the information fed to me.

Gossiping and guessing bring sorrow, heaviness and distrust. These are the very things I am making efforts to overcome. Poison can come in many disguises, but poison is poison whether from an enemy or a friend.

The unlimited family

In a family I know that some of the members may have certain faults and shortcomings, but it is usually very easy to overlook them because, after all, they are of the same blood and we have grown up together. Although I may be able to tolerate a certain weakness in a brother or sister, I will refuse to put up with the same failing when it manifests itself outside of my close family circle.

I now realise that the world is an extended family. Taking it a step further, I understand that we share a common parent, the Supreme Soul, God. To have deep love for God as the parent of all souls makes it very easy to have love for all souls, regardless of the colour, caste, race or creed.

There's freedom at the roots

There is now a heightened consciousness of "Who am I?" and an eager curiosity to delve into the beginnings of that existence. In this age of alienation and fragmentation, I long for real belonging and retrace my steps, hoping for signals that would welcome me back to roots.

To return to roots has many different interpretations. To some, it means a homeland, a place of belonging and stability. To others it means the return to everything that is noble and dignifying, both in the external and internal expressions. It is a search for enrichment. To still some others, it means a journey towards the basic intrinsic worth. A quest for immortality.

A return to roots. A return to the source. Whatever the reason for this search, whatever the motivation, the yearnings are the same.

At the roots I yearn to find a taste of my eternity. At the roots I hope to find rejuvenation and sustenance to maintain me in whatever position I presently find myself. At the roots, there is no more search. At the roots, there is no more yearning. Only freedom to be forever.

*H*umility in greatness

Greatness! It is a powerful motivating force. I cannot think of anyone that does not want to show their worth, or display those qualities that distinguish them from the ordinary. Everyone wants to be somebody. Everyone wants to shine.

It is with this consciousness that I aspire and seek position and wealth, power and fame. Every action, every gesture is performed with the aim of becoming the greatest. But often in my quest to fulfil this urge, this desire for greatness, I display many qualities that are less, very much less than great. I compete, I rival, I become jealous and envious, and sometimes I even end up with intense feelings of hatred because I think that others are preventing me from realising the greatness I deserve. I stain my greatness.

With much effort and striving I finally attain the goal. I achieve the championship. I have acquired greatness. I strut, I brag, I boast; I become extravagant and arrogant. I am totally egotistic in my greatness, and again the greatness is stained. I have missed the fine subtlety and essence of greatness for, in spite of my several achievements due to position, service, qualities, blood connections, championship etc., my true nobility and greatness lie in my modesty and humility.

The one with humility wins the heart and co-operation of others.

Set the goal, then aim for it

Everyone feels the need to improve himself. Words alone cannot bring about transformation. Words only convey information. It is the practical application or use of that information that will bring about change.

If I desire to improve myself in any way at all, I must first recognise the need for improvement. For example, if I think that I want to give up smoking and I have the deep desire to stop, then that is half the battle already won. I will seek out a suitable method and apply myself to it wholeheartedly. Victory comes automatically. On the other hand, however, if there is only the feeling that I should stop, but not the firm aim, then no matter how many methods I adopt, success will be nothing more than an illusion, and so to kick the habit seems an impossible task.

So firstly I establish my aim, and then maintain effort along those lines. I recognise the need, and automatically the ways and means will make themselves available to me.

Influencing the atmosphere

Thoughts are very powerful. It is thought power that creates an atmosphere in a room. The atmosphere may or may not be uplifting depending on the thoughts of those in the room. If I can control my mind and develop its positive power, I can influence rather than be influenced by the atmosphere around me. My dependence on others and physical things will decrease. I will gain contentment, and within that contentment there will be great strength. Then nothing will be experienced as difficult. The question of wanting to drop out of the system or escape does not arise because, although I remain within society, in my thoughts I am beyond its influence.

Experiencing myself as a soul, a spiritual being, and seeing all others in the same way as souls, children of the one God, and by turning my thoughts towards God's unlimited qualities, there is a gradual change in my thought patterns.

Am I living the way I should?

I cannot know the deep and most beautiful experiences of joy while my thoughts and vision are trapped within the dark grey walls of body-consciousness. In words I may rejoice, but do my actions really reveal my beliefs? Am I living my life in accordance with the teachings I follow, whether it be Christianity, Hinduism, Islam, Buddhism, Judaism, or whatever? Am I adopting spirituality in my dealings with others?

Spirituality does not mean sitting in a church or temple 24 hours a day. It means living in the awareness that I, the soul, am a spiritual being, the child of God, and that all souls are my sisters and brothers.

Spirituality means a life with values based on truth rather than the acquisition of objects; a life in which I can understand and appreciate the importance of developing good qualities within myself: divine virtues such as tolerance, co-operation, love etc; a life in which I can communicate and relate to others with a smile in my eyes and happiness in my voice; a life in which my aim does not have four wheels, but my aim is to make the best of the life I am living and to be honest with myself, honest with God and truthful in my dealings with others.

Aiming for complete tolerance

How much tolerance should I have? This is a question asked by many. It is a deep one. If I say that I have been tolerating a particular situation for such and such a time and now I must react, this means that I do not have the power of tolerance. I may have the nature of being tolerant, but only up to a certain point. I do not have the power.

Power means total control. Therefore, it should be unlimited. Tolerance should be complete. This is a very important power to develop in this world at present. Tolerance means to endure all difficulties with love and humility. Everyone has to face problems and situations of all sorts, but everything depends on the way in which the soul faces them. Since every situation must be faced, why not face it in the consciousness of love? If I keep asking myself the question of how and why so-and-so is behaving in this way, this will destroy the power of tolerance. I must realise that every soul is unique in personality and qualities.

If I remember this constantly, the power of tolerance will become easy to inculcate. Others will eventually come to see my point and accept help or advice. But sometimes the fruits of tolerance take a long time to manifest themselves.

Inner plumbing

I recently had a huge bill for some plumbing work done in my kitchen. All the grease and grime had accumulated and settled firmly in the pipes. They blocked the flow of water, and everything became clogged. I had not realised this was happening. There was a back flow, a foul smell and total stagnation. It was a scene of total chaos. The plumber extracted the dues, and I vowed never to allow my drainage system to become clogged again.

Often I walk around with my spiritual system clogged and blocked up. This is evident from my mean actions and thoughts, from my despair and frustration and lack of hope. What is the alloy, the foreign matter, that has entered my spiritual stream and clogged it? In my plumbing I know without hesitation that it is the grease and grime, but what is the parallel in my spiritual system?

The grease and grime that block my spiritual flow are the feelings of greed, ego, anger, hatred, lust and attachment. These vices stick firmly to me and become so fixed that I assume them to be part of my personality. I think it's natural to be jealous, hateful and full of pride. But is it? Is that my natural, original state? Or did I, like the plumbing example, start out with pure, clean and unclogged fixtures?

My most permanent fixture is the soul. My original nature is purity and peace. If I find myself in a state of impurity and peacelessness, then I know that something is wrong and that I have moved away from my perfect stage. Then I need to start the declogging and the purification process so that I can return to my original state.

Give respect to get respect

Someone has not acted according to what I expected. They have been slight in their behaviour towards me. They have ignored me or been short in their responses. I feel that I have not been given the proper respect that I deserve. I feel put down.

What are my feelings towards myself? How do I behave towards myself? Do I always remain in the high state of self-respect, and create thoughts that are elevated and pure? Are my actions noble and beyond ulterior motives? Are my words always soothing and uplifting? Or are they of the degrading and cutting-down variety? How is my self-respect?

It is always easy to expect and demand respect from others. It is simple to criticise others for not being respectful or for being rude or for not showing the proper appreciation. It is difficult to ask respect from myself.

Without self-respect I can never gain respect from others. Without self-respect I will always be performing self-defeating actions. Without self-respect I will always be looking outside myself and will constantly be at the whims and fancies of other people's dispositions. I cannot get respect by asking for it. I only receive it when I give it to myself and to others.

Thoughts are the nucleus

I know how important thoughts are. Thoughts are the nucleus from which every action, every vibration springs. Thoughts shape our world. Thoughts are fertilised by knowledge. A person with a certain kind of knowledge usually creates thoughts in harmony with that knowledge. Knowledge gives wisdom; a person without knowledge is a person whose thoughts will be formed in ignorance.

Before people had correct knowledge of the shape of the world, they thought that it was flat. Think how this thought, based on incorrect knowledge, must have affected people's lives. No doubt belief systems must have evolved around this thought. Cultural patterns, attitudes and expression must have been clearly influenced by this incorrect knowledge. Moreover, the incorrect thinking was not just isolated to one individual or a group of individuals, it was mass popular thinking. Perhaps it is mass ignorance.

Today I also live in a world where there is inaccurate, incorrect and inadequate knowledge. Many people still have improper knowledge of themselves, of their destiny, of their purpose in life and of God. These misconceptions lead them to a life of improper action based on improper thoughts.

One of the aspects of knowledge most lacking in today's world is that of self. To explore and define oneself only in terms of the physical is a great error. To think that I am only my body is to be body-conscious. To be body-conscious means to express my whole life on the basis of inaccurate perceptions based on incorrect knowledge.

I am an important actor in life's drama

Have I ever stopped to think how important I am? Did I wake this morning with firm resolutions to play my part in life to the best of my ability? The whole of human history is like an unlimited drama, and each of us has our unique role to play.

In an ordinary play there are understudies, but in this play of life, out of the five and a half billion actors on the stage, not one of them can play my role better than I. I am a very special person. No one's role is more important than the other; some may appear to be more significant, but each has its own beauty and very specific purpose.

Take the example of a motor car. My car may have cost thousands of dollars, but if my spark plugs which cost but a few dollars are not sparking, then my flashy, speedy car will not move an inch, unless of course, I push it. The other point to remember is that a spark plug cannot be used in place of a water pump, and a gear box cannot play the part of a radiator. Each has its own speciality and reason for being. Only when I understand my role in life and play it with attention and accuracy can I experience contentment and a mind free of jealousy.

Ego is so subtle

Ego is one of the most subtle feelings I can ever experience. All other vices need something or someone else with whom to react or interact, but ego needs nothing except myself. So easily I get caught up with myself and what I regard as my own importance that I lose sight of everything else around me. I become so pompous. The expression "swollen with pride" is a very accurate description of someone under the influence of ego. I become so distorted that the only vision is the vision of the self. As a result, I never give regard to anyone else. I never have respect for other people's ideas and opinions.

Obviously this will create friction. As I do not give any regard to the ideas of others, they become annoyed at my attitude towards them, and so they in turn react and become unco-operative. Because I am so puffed up with ego, I then ask myself what I have done to create their negativity towards me. I have done nothing to them.

Confidence leads me to victory

What is the state of my confidence today? Am I intact and courageously facing the scenes of drama as they unfold in day-to-day activities, or am I tattered like a leaf that the insects have attacked? Am I even afraid to go ahead in case some vermin, real or imaginary, attack and tear me to pieces even more?

It is very easy to lose confidence in myself, confidence in others, confidence in institutions and upheld value systems. My confidence slowly vanishes. The present does not project a good future, and it is this fear of the uncertainty of the future that sometimes makes us lose confidence in life generally.

I may not be able to control the various circumstances of life and I may not be able to change any of the existing systems and "ocracies" by which I am surrounded, but one thing, one very important aspect lies within my control. That is I, that individual, that separate and distinct entity called the person, who can control, change, mould and create a future that is bright for me.

When I become introspective and start working to cultivate the garden within myself, I get to know and recognise my real being, my real existence, my real purpose for living. In this awareness and experience, I become filled with a confidence that is not easily bitten by the worms of circumstances. It is a confidence that is worm-resistant because it is a confidence nurtured in the truth of God and self. With a strong union and relationship between these two, self and God, I will always be victorious. Confidence in the self enables me to carry on. Confidence in God leads to victory.

My words reflect the inner self

Words! They are all around me! I see them, I hear them, I use them. Harsh words, soothing words, biting words; words that give pain and sorrow; words that give joy and pleasure. They are vital to communication.

When words are spoken there are reactions, negative or positive. Either thoughts are triggered or emotions fired or actions performed. Words colour our behaviour. And how lovely it is to hear words that are calm and free from rancour and aggression. To hear words that lift the soul and leave it with renewed vigour. Such words are the sparks of purity.

It is important to remember that my speech indicates what is in my mind. As the thinking, so the words uttered. Mental calmness makes my words calm. A pure mind makes for pure words. It is said that speech may exalt someone to kingship or send him to the gallows. I should never let myself indulge in false, bitter and vicious speech. My words should reflect my true, inner nature, that of purity and peace. Words, once spoken, can never be recalled. They reverberate all around, beyond our control.

Today, as I utter words, what effect will they have on those who hear them? Will they be the words that are poisonous and cause pain? Or will my tongue be like that of the nightingale, sweet and so, so very soothing and lovely to the ear?

The world judges me by my actions

Actions are the results of thoughts, and thoughts reveal themselves through actions. It is through actions that the world assesses me. People think of me as responsible or irresponsible, kind or harsh, benevolent or miserly etc.

Actions plant the seeds of my future. As an old proverb states: "If I sow nettles, I cannot reap roses". So whatever the reaction, it will be the result of that action. The results of actions can be swift, manifesting themselves immediately, or delayed, taking a longer time to become apparent. Swift or delayed, the results are sure to be evidenced.

It is according to my actions that the world reacts to me. If I perform angry actions, I get angry reactions. If I perform peaceful actions, the results are peaceful.

If through my actions I am creating my fortune or misfortune, it would be in my best interests to monitor the quality of my actions.

Let all actions be pure. That is, free from vicious motives. Let all actions be for building up instead of tearing down. Let actions be such that, no matter how long the period of germination and growth, I can always be contented and happy with the present, knowing that the future will only hold joy.

Eyes for pearls of truth

There is an old story about two types of birds. The crow is the type of bird that sees only the dirt and filth. Wherever there is rubbish, I find the crow feasting noisily. Then there is the swan. The swan is most selective. It sees only the gems and virtues. If there are pearls and pebbles, the swan selects the pearls. If there is milk and water, the swan chooses the milk. What a difference between these two birds - one feeding on the vices and rubbish, the other feasting on the virtues and gems.

Today there are crow-like as well as swan-like characteristics among the people of the world. To gossip, to lie, to speak evil, to use vile language as well as to listen to these, is to have crow-like characteristics. To speak truth and purity, to use only the uplifting and worthwhile and to hear only the uplifting and worthwhile, is to have the characteristics of a swan.

Strength and courage for truth

Every action has an equal and opposite reaction. Whatever I do, when all is said and done, I do for or to myself. Perhaps I should think before I perform actions because after the seed of action is sown I have to reap the fruit. Moreover, I do not receive only one fruit for every seed sown; I often get a whole crop, good or bad according to the action or seed.

What scale do I use to assess right from wrong? Do I have one scale that is constantly accurate and stable, or do I change scales to suit my changing moods? Sometimes my vision is clouded with the dust of anger, greed, pride etc., and so I am not able to read the scale accurately. And sometimes I know what I should be doing; I realise that an action is wrong, but I have neither the strength nor the courage to accept the reading of the scale of judgement, and I go ahead and make the most appalling mistakes time and time again.

So it would appear that the greatest need is to find a source that will instill within me that strength and courage to enable me not just to see what is right, but to put that right into action. That source is God.

Happiness

Am I happy or sad today? If there is any sadness I make a strong effort to be free of it quickly, otherwise it grows like a vine in the rainy season: by midday I will be confused; by evening a whole jungle of weak, wasteful and negative attitudes will have taken deep roots in my mind. The result equals chaos.

Sometimes I reach a stage where the attitude is: "So what if I feel the blues today? It is my life; I can feel how I want to feel; no one else will be affected". Firstly, the more I allow myself to experience sorrow, the less time I have available to be happy and contented. It sounds ridiculously obvious, but am I aware of the value of happiness? It is an extremely rare commodity, and the cost goes sky high.

Secondly, is it my life? Yes, I am living it, but am I not a member of a family or a co-worker with others, and am I not part of society? If so, then every movement affects and is affected by those around me.

Everything happens in its season

A calamity that appears today will sooner or later disappear. After all, nothing that belongs to this world or happens here is everlasting. A person who is exceptionally cruel today may later on, due to some serious circumstances, be moved to kindness.

If I remain in a stage of patience, it helps me to understand why events were delayed and to avoid making the same mistakes in the future.

If I am too anxious for the results of something to come about, it is just like trying to eat unripe fruit. Time will change me and everything around me, but I cannot change time, so why get myself upset and annoyed? Everything happens according to its own time and season. I cannot hope to pick mangoes out of season when the tree has not even flowered, but there is much enjoyment in tasting the first fruit of the season. Am I so arrogant that I feel everything and everyone else must fit into my timetable? Am I so foolish as to believe that my life and state of mind are an accurate yardstick by which everything else can be assessed and judged?

It would be good to realise that each of us is different and to adjust to the ever-changing scenes of life. I must learn to accept as well as appreciate those differences, and mould myself accordingly.

In the drama of life everyone has a part

When I compare myself with other human beings, the result will be either jealousy or ego. If I feel they are better than me, there will be such resentment that I cannot wait for them to put a foot wrong so that I can be given the opportunity of pointing out their weakness to others. Or, on the other hand, I may feel so inferior that I become depressed. If I compare myself with others and I feel I am better than they, ego will appear. This of course brings in a whole series of negative feelings.

So, bearing in mind the variety of human souls, each with their part to play, I am saved from such feelings. Why? Because very quietly I become aware that, unlike a drama in a theatre where there can be an understudy or substitute, in this unlimited drama of life there is no other actor, no other soul who has the ability or knowledge to play my part.

My part is completely unique and individual. On a larger scale there have to be many different types of people within the world, and each has a rightful place.

$\mathcal{B}e$ careful of what I feed the intellect

It is a most satisfying experience to listen to someone whose intellect is clear and sparkling. To observe the rhythm of words, the natural sequence of thoughts, the reasoning power, the authority and yet the simplicity of language displayed by such an intellect is a joy. The experience is thrilling and refreshing.

Is it a natural endowment? If not, is it difficult to acquire or cultivate?

Let me explore. The intellect, like the organs of the body, is not a stagnant mass. It is alive and subject to growth, non-growth, over-growth and even pollution and decay. The intellect, then, must be treated with respect and given careful attention.

With much concern and care I exercise muscles, groom my hair and even guard my teeth against tooth decay. As I am careful about the food with which I nourish my body, so must I watch the nourishment with which I feed the intellect. Do I feed my intellect rubbish? Do I constantly churn nonsense, non-essentials and obscenities? Such thoughts poison the intellect and make it murky, stagnant and sluggish. To make my intellect clear, I must constantly create clean, nourishing thoughts.

Different strokes for different folks

Authority often acts as an obstacle for people trying to find common ground or a mutual level of communication.

I was at one time on the same level as my colleagues at work, but being suddenly promoted I became intoxicated. I used this new authority to prove myself, usually at the cost of those beneath me.

If I did not speak to someone in the correct manner, I would receive an equally unsatisfactory reaction. People became hostile or even defensive. Inevitably, my efforts to communicate would be seriously hampered. Everyone could not be treated in the same manner. Some needed to be encouraged and inspired. Others needed to feel that I could trust them to perform a particular task.

When I am in a position of authority, it is vital that I understand the intention of the person to whom I am attempting to relate. A little like dialling a phone number. No matter how badly I want to get through to someone, unless I dial the correct number, there is no way that communication can take place. In this case, I must understand that every person has an individual set of emotional tendencies, personality traits, prejudices etc.

Therefore, in order to maintain harmonious relationships, I must give regard and consideration to the feelings of others.

No stronger foundation than truth

It seems easy to think negative thoughts and act in a negative way. On an individual level, I find that past events in my life leave impressions on me that form and shape my character and personality. Very often the painful lessons that I should learn from leave me tired, hopeless and bitter. I concentrate on the pain and forget about learning the valuable lesson, so all benefit is lost. Therefore when life presents me with so many lessons and tests, the impressions left colour my thoughts, and I experience thoughts of doubt, fear, hatred and anger.

On a collective level, everyone is contributing to the negative atmosphere by creating and harbouring a multitude of waste and negative thoughts and attitudes. In turn this negative atmosphere can, and usually does, influence the individual. So it is a vicious circle. To break out of it requires strength and determination, otherwise in a negative and impure world it appears quite natural and normal to be negative and impure. When I make efforts for purity and a positive attitude I may encounter opposition, but I remember that anything with a foundation in falsehood cannot and will not last. Only that which has a strong foundation will last.

There can be no stronger foundation than truth. Truth may sometimes be hidden, but it is eternal and will always reveal itself at the correct time.

Don't run with the crowd

I need to feel a part of the whole; however, the way in which I function is dependent, all too often, on the influence of other people. I lack that inner strength and courage to be able to make my own decisions. It is far easier to move with the crowd than to choose my own direction. But is the crowd always right? Can I justify a wrong act by counting the number of people performing that act?

There seems to be a great deal of duality within me. I do not want to feel left out, but yet there are many things I disagree with which are alien to my nature. I know that peace is important, and yet I give support to peaceless and violent activities. I understand the value of happiness, but I cling with mindless abandon to that which causes sorrow. Anyway, who wants to be singled out as being different, as being weird?

To see what is right and not to do ... is this how I want to live? Can I experience true stability if my mind tells me one thing and I do something else? I try to gather my thoughts every now and then, and to see what strength there is in virtue and how much virtue in strength of thought. I ask myself what I really want, that which is perishable or imperishable? The choice is mine.

Lean on a stable pillar

"We all need someone to lean on". How often have I heard that expression? It is of course very true. Another such saying is, "A problem shared is a problem halved".

It is interesting that sometimes I lean on someone, and in my selfishness I do not realise how much harm I am causing to that person. If I weigh 200 pounds and sit on a broken chair, the chair will break. Most people have so many problems and burdens of their own, but due to friendship they will lend an ear and help me with my load. However, this in turn makes them weaker and weaker with the result that our relationship becomes strained. It is good to share a problem, but I must take care that the one I am speaking to is strong enough to shoulder it, otherwise I will be doing a great disservice to that person.

If I want someone to lean on, it is good to remember that God is the most stable pillar you will ever find.

Whilst I enjoy talking and airing views with my friends, it is necessary to be merciful to those who are showing me mercy. To hand over my burden to someone else, and then to see them struggle under the weight, is not an ideal situation. And if I am on the receiving end and I wish to help someone with their burden, it is worth remembering that all people are limited in their capacity to help others. It is far better to help a soul come closer to God; then all help is received.

The beauty in helping out

How important is it to co-operate with others? Examining the state of the world, it can be seen that co-operation is a word widely used but not so widely practised.

There are reasons for this; one of them is uncertainty about my own position or role. Because I do not have firm faith in myself, I develop a possessive attitude towards whatever I do; and not only do I avoid co-operating with others, but I do not allow anyone else to co-operate with me just in case that person becomes too clever and is able to do a better job.

Sometimes I avoid lending a hand quite simply because I am not able to work in harmony with others. It seems strange that human beings, children of one God, should find difficulty in working with each other. When I come to know myself, my capabilities, my limitations and my role, there is then no problem about finding harmony with those around me. For I understand that, if something needs to be done properly, I should use the best hands available. It has been said, "No person is an island".

Time and patience have their reward

I have been programmed into wanting everything right now, this moment, not a second later. I just cannot wait for anything. Science and technology have made everything instant and immediate. I want a high position at work, but am not prepared to go through the hardship of climbing the ladder of success; instead I search for an elevator. I want to be loved and have my ideas respected, but find it difficult to give love or respect to the ideas of others.

To carve a beautiful statue, the sculptor has to hammer and chisel away at the stone. Everything requires efforts, and it is those very efforts that endow me with the qualification for holding the position I desire or even for seeing my "dream come true". It is those very hardships that give me the strength to go ahead and the determination to succeed.

Without the pitfalls, how would I be able to value my achievement? If fruit simply falls from the tree, I discard it as rotten fruit. When I pick it myself, it seems so sweet. It is the hour of trial that makes me great, not the hour of triumph.

Peace of mind - my prized possession

Is it possible to remain peaceful if someone destroys one of my prized possessions?

What is to be gained from losing my peaceful nature, and what benefit is there in acting in a calm and rational way? If I have all the wealth I desire, name, fame and glory, yet am without health, happiness and peace of mind, can I enjoy that wealth? And what value does it really have if I cannot enjoy it? Peace of mind is one of my most prized possessions. I may spend my whole life looking for it, yet I will allow the most minor incident to rob me of whatever little peace I may possess.

If I succumb to anger, then just observe how much energy is being used in a destructive manner. Why not use that energy creatively? If something has been taken from me, instead I try to learn the appropriate lesson and move ahead. My anger or tears will not resolve the situation.

Which role is really me?

I often marvel at the number and variety of roles I have to play every day; did I ever stop to wonder which one is really me? From the moment I wake my actions begin, and so I become the actor. I can play the part of a spouse, parent or child while at home for the first few hours of the morning. After leaving home and arriving at work, there are more roles for me to play: friend, employee, colleague, wheeler-dealer, counsellor, decision-maker, etc. Then in the evening I can play the part of a committee member or sports spectator, and then I return home to my family role once again. Which one of these am I really?

To realise that I am a soul, a spiritual being, and that my body is just like a costume through which I play my part on this unlimited drama stage of life makes things a little clearer. My costume, the body, goes through different stages as time goes by, and so my part changes also, but I remain the spiritual being, conscient energy with my true original nature of peace and purity.

Even though I may not be at peace now, it is possible to experience that peace by thinking, speaking and performing actions in a pure and peaceful manner. Then I will come to know what it is like to be me.

Every morning, upon waking and having sweet conversation with God, I remember that I am a spiritual being, an actor, originally peaceful and pure. Establishing this consciousness at the beginning of the day helps me to experience myself as I truly am, and then I can perform all the roles of my day with ease and enjoyment.

*A*m I getting soul power?

I am hungry for power. There are many forms of power that I crave, but how often do I seek to have power over myself? Having power over others is artificial and limited. When I have power and control over myself, then I am able to empower others. What is the value of having some special power if I lack the ability to tolerate others? Is physical power of value if I cannot co-operate with others?

The body and other physical objects are perishable and therefore temporary, whereas the soul is eternal and imperishable. The power, strength and beauty of personality that come from developing virtues are indelible. Are we paying attention to things that give power to the soul, the power of personality?

My next step depends on my last

Each step I have taken in life so far, whether good or bad, has led me to my present position. The plus factors as well as the minus marks are all taken into account. Although I am aware of the past, I cannot really know the future.

The only thing that separates the past from the future is the present, and I do know what is happening at present. What is past is surely past, but if I have learnt my lessons well the past can remain the past. I will correct any mistakes at the present so that the future can be positive.

The present moment is the foundation for the next moment. The way in which I act or react to a situation now determines the way I will act in the future. If I allow something to irritate me today I may well lose my temper over it tomorrow. However, if attention is paid to being positive, powerful and loving today, then tomorrow I will be able to handle any situation.

The biggest mistake

The fear of making mistakes very often causes mistakes. Here I am at the crossroads, not sure which way to go. I may ask others for directions, but ultimately the decision is mine. So we gather together all the facts and try to see down the road a little before finally making a decision.

But then comes hesitation as I doubt myself and worry about the future, with the result that time goes by. And as time goes by, the decision gets harder and more questions arise. I stand confused at the crossroads, and fear sets in. Fear and confusion are two killers. They kill my courage and confidence and my clarity of vision.

When I realise the value of time, the first decision I make is to not waste a single second. In this way I save myself from anxiety. I must be prepared, however, to face the consequences of my judgement, taking whatever comes as my doing. If I find that I have made the right decision it is good, but if it turns out to be wrong, then I must make corrections and press on towards the destination with courage.

The biggest mistake is to live in fear of making a mistake.

I can learn from my mistakes

A friend asked me recently whether if I had to live my life over again I would change anything. My immediate response was: why should I want to change anything? My friend and I both knew that I had made some wrong decisions in my life, and that paying the penalty was rough.

By looking at life and seeing not only the past, but also the present and future, I realise that in order to grow and progress, meeting the challenges of the present, I have to learn to run the obstacle race.

It is not that I can jump every obstacle successfully the first time. Sometimes a couple of attempts are needed to clear the hurdle. I feel pain as I hit my shins, but hopefully I will learn how to jump properly the next time.

If I look at life positively as a game or drama, it is clear that I cannot choose what scenes I have to play in, so I should be prepared to play my part to the best of my ability under all circumstances. As I play my part I learn how to improve my act. The variety scenes in the drama give me an opportunity to become versatile and flexible, and to gain strength from the trials.

I find beauty when I develop the soul

When people spend much time and energy on developing their bodies and making them attractive to other people, is there ever the thought to develop the soul and make it attractive to God?

The body is made of physical matter and is subject to ageing, to changes in temperature and to death. If I have a beautiful body now, there is no guarantee that it will remain so for more than a few years.

And suppose I should be involved in an accident and lose a limb, or suffer great facial injuries resulting in permanent scars; that physical beauty will be lost. In fact, everything which is physical has a limit; the body must perish.

The soul is an eternal, immortal point of spiritual light. The soul does not die. Within the soul there are impressions which form my personality. If I take steps to develop the soul and feed it with spiritual knowledge, my character, my personality, can become rich and full of beauty.

This will enable me to attain my full potential so that I can be an instrument to help other souls. This is true beauty.

Use mental energy wisely

While I wait at the bus stop or traffic lights, what is going through my mind? While I am bathing or cooking food, what type of thoughts am I having? I sometimes check myself: "What am I thinking?"

At a time when world resources are at their lowest, and people working towards conserving energy, am I throwing away enormous quantities of thought energy by the second?

When I use up a lot of physical energy, my body becomes fatigued. In exactly the same way, by expending large quantities of mental energy the mind gets tired, giving rise to frustration, boredom, tension, etc. When my mind is tired and fatigued, every task becomes difficult.

It is good to examine myself and see just where my energy is being lost. Even if I eat well and nourish my body with care, I may still find myself feeling tired and worn out if I do not use my mental energy wisely.

Cheerfulness

Cheerfulness is a quality that I like. The one who possesses it becomes like a magnet of goodwill. I strive to attain some measure of this quality.

Cheerfulness comes from a sense of well-being and contentment. It is an elevated quality, but it does not always stay with me. Many circumstances and events come and steal my happiness and joy. I make mistakes, I worry, become agitated and sorrowful. Thoughts of envy and jealousy, anger and hatred enter the mind, and my cheerfulness vanishes.

To find cheerfulness and inner contentment, all I need to do is focus on the good qualities I see in others. Leave the bad qualities aside. When I see bad qualities, when I retain all the rubbish, the defects of others poison my intellect. Why harbour negative thoughts? The results of these cause undue sorrow, and again I lose my cheerfulness.

Thoughts are the source of my actions. When I focus on good qualities, my thoughts will be pure and my actions will be elevated, bringing with them the result of great joy, contentment, happiness and a face of cheerfulness.

Image of success

I once met a very successful couple.

There was no pomp and no ceremony. They rarely spoke of themselves, and yet their every action exuded knowledge and self-confidence. Their manners were soft and unaggressive. They seemed to understand their relationship with others and with the environment through their expression of sympathetic listening and quiet, peaceful interactions.

These individuals were given much regard and respect although they never sought it.

They were accepted and appreciated as beings who displayed an elevated consciousness by wearing their success with humility.

After meeting them, I felt empowered.

The Brahma Kumaris Centres
in the United Kingdom and Ireland

London
Global Co-operation House, 65 Pound Lane, London NW10 2HH
Phone; 0181 459 1400

Nuneham Courtenay
Global Retreat Centre, Nuneham Park, Nuneham Courtenay,
Oxon OX44 9PG
Phone; 01865 343 551

Edinburgh
20 Polwarth Crescent, Edinburgh, EH11 1HW
Phone; 0131 229 7220

Cardiff
15 Morlais Street, Roath Park, Cardiff, CF2 5HQ
Phone; 01222 480 557

Dublin, Ireland
36 Lansdowne Road, Ballsbridge, Dublin 4, Ireland
Phone; (353) 1603 967

Introductory courses in meditation are offered at each of our
centres throughout the country, free of charge.
For more information and the address of a centre near you,
please contact one of the above centres.